A Piece of Cake
The Gallery

A Piece of Cake
The Gallery

Heidi and Karlo

Copyright © 2012, Heidi and Karlo

All rights reserved. No part of this book may be reproduced, stored, or transmitted by any means—whether auditory, graphic, mechanical, or electronic—without written permission of both publisher and author, except in the case of brief excerpts used in critical articles and reviews. Unauthorized reproduction of any part of this work is illegal and is punishable by law.

ISBN 978-0-9873985-0-5

Special Occasion

A Piece of Cake The Gallery

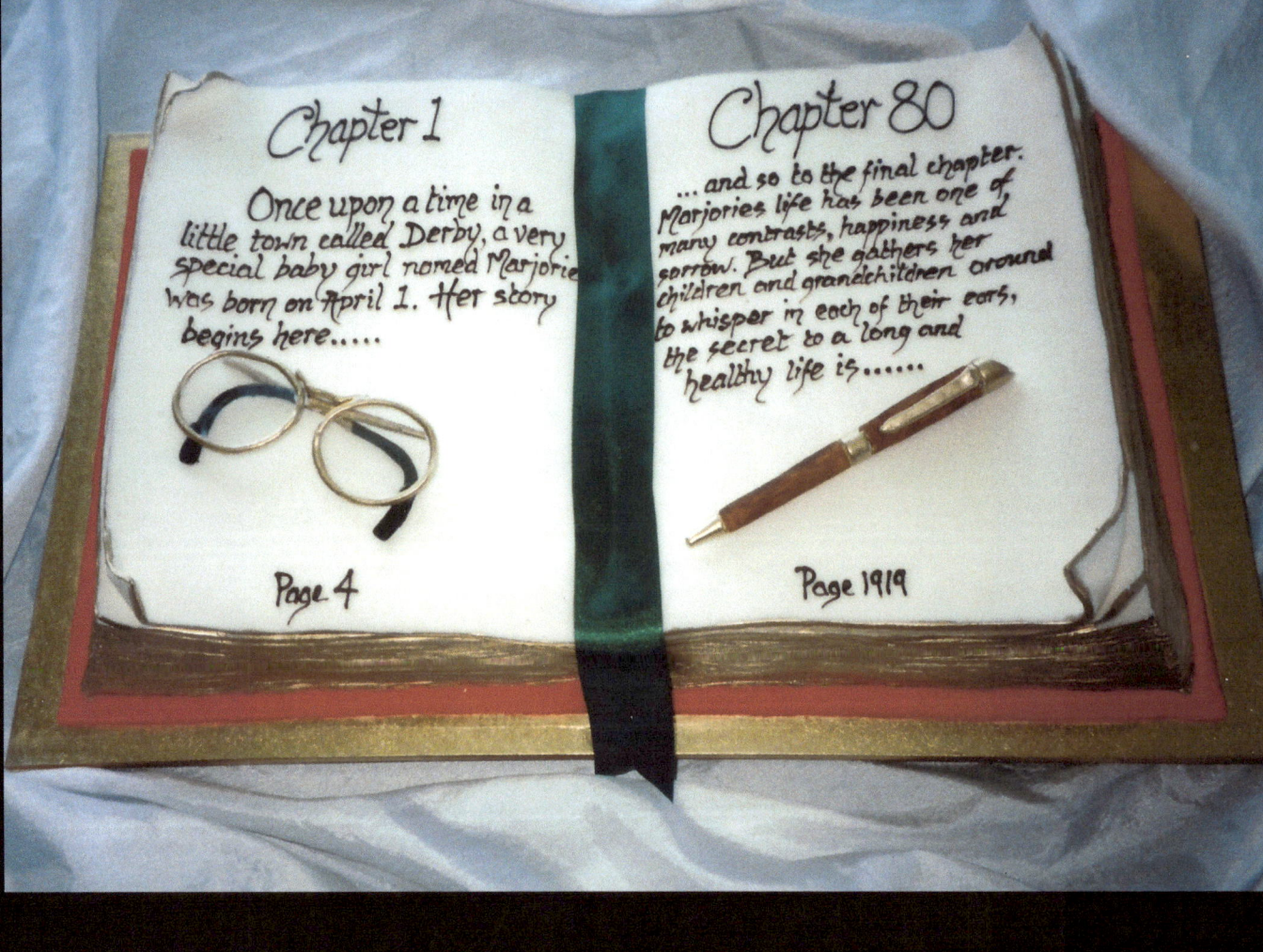

Heidi and Karlo

AUNTY DOTS
PFAFF
PFAFF
Gary
Happy 65
60th or
whatever
birthday

Heidi and Karlo

I'm Not Aging
I'm ripening to perfection

Happy 5th Birthday Emily

Heidi and Karlo

A Piece of Cake The Gallery

A Piece of Cake The Gallery

Wedding

Heidi and Karlo

Heidi and Karlo

A Piece of Cake The Gallery

Heidi and Karlo

Cake The Gallery

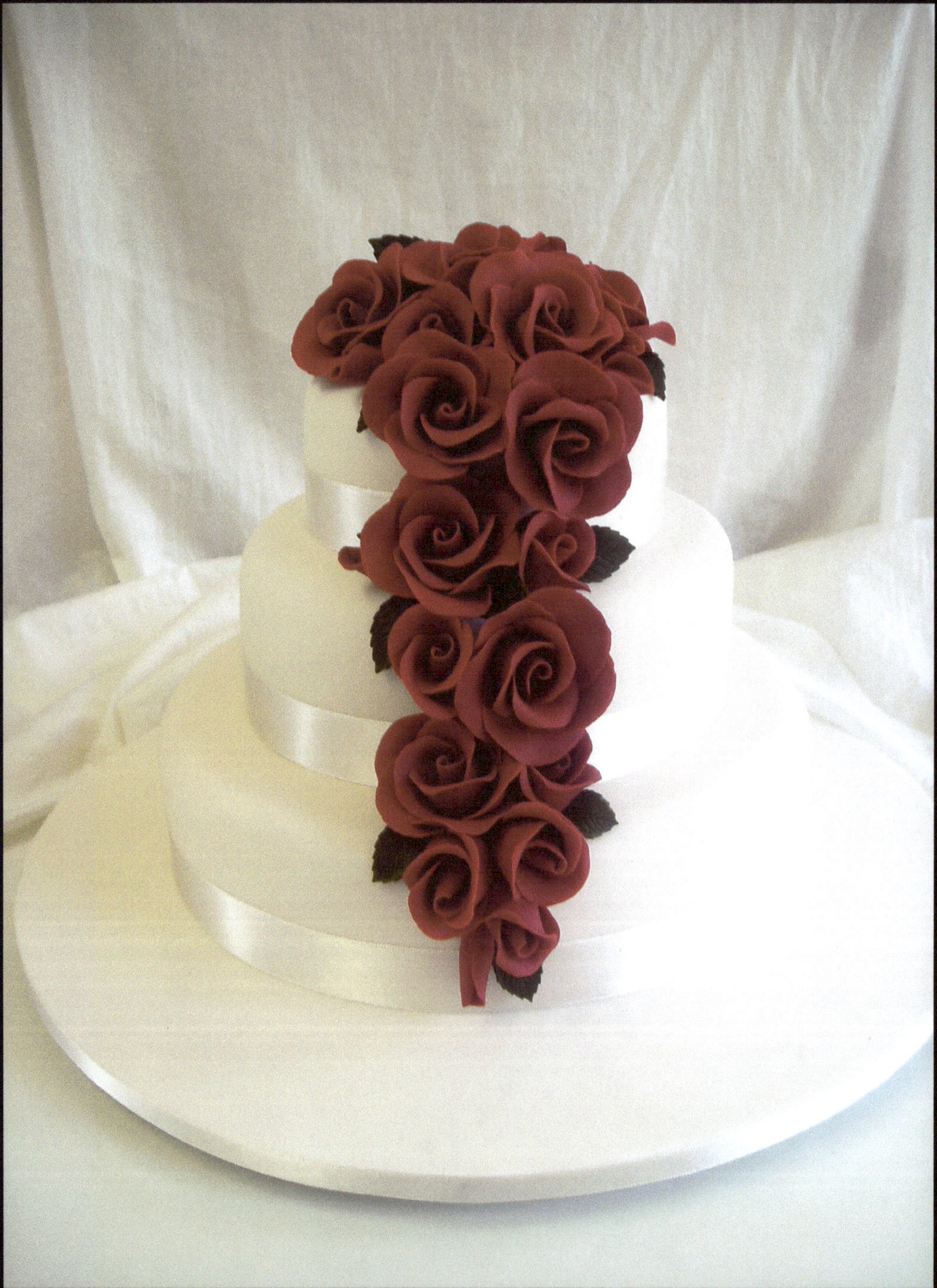

Heidi and Karlo

Heidi and Karlo

Heidi and Karlo

A Piece of Cake The Gallery

A Piece of Cake The Gallery

Heidi and Karlo

Heidi and Karlo

Heidi and Karlo

www.ingramcontent.com/pod-product-compliance
Lightning Source LLC
Chambersburg PA
CBHW041522220426
43669CB00002B/24